Child of

Child of Stalin

Foreword:

Based on true life accounts

We often see one of two scenarios when it comes to important judicial decisions:

Someone can, who is clearly a person who has committed heinous crimes and caused untold sorrow get clean away with what they have done or conversely another individual after 20 years in jail is freed on DNA evidence after having been fitted up by the police in a miscarriage of justice case such as Derek Bentley, hanged for committing a murder while he was under arrest at the time and not having pulled the trigger and having the intelligence of a 10-year old.

These injustices are taking place today at the hands of Magistrates and Crown Court Judges and yet no one seems to be held to account for their biassed judgements.

This paperback has been written in an effort to highlight a single example of the extreme bias focused upon one individual from his childhood years until his adult life, due to his near unpronounceable name, his social standing, refugee misfit of a father and his schizophrenic mother, formulating a cocktail of a social dynamic that would be rife for the authorities to exploit by way of their harsh judicial bias.

This paperback attempts to finally disclose a situation where this judicial system had backfired upon itself and left a record where one of its targets had not succumbed to its sense of power and uprightness, but simply kept a log of the occasions where he can expose their misgivings.

Imagine, for a moment, a fair and impartial supreme judge with the authority to finally call to account these judges within the establishment who have abused their position as the following occurs:

The grand chamber stands in solemnity, its atmosphere heavy with anticipation as the ultimate arbiter takes his place within a court to judge the courts. Amidst the hushed murmurs of the assembly, the voice of the supreme judge resonates with authority, piercing through the stillness.

"How long," he begins, his gaze sweeping across the gathered "judges," "will you persist in defending the unjust, and in showing favouritism to the wicked?"

His words hang in the air, a stern rebuke directed at those entrusted with the solemn duty of dispensing justice. For too long, they have turned a blind eye to the cries of the oppressed, preferring instead to align themselves with the powerful and corrupt.

"For a change, defend the weak and the fatherless," he commands, his voice echoing with conviction. "Uphold the cause of the poor and the oppressed. Rescue the vulnerable from the clutches of the wicked."

It is a clarion call to rightness, a reminder of the obligation borne by those in positions of authority. Yet, despite the gravity of his words, the "judges" remain unmoved, their hearts hardened by self-interest and complacency.

"You 'judges' are blind," he declares, his tone laced with sorrow. "You stumble in darkness, oblivious to the crumbling foundations of society."

He sees through their pretence, their façade of wisdom crumbling under the weight of their ignorance. No longer can they claim ignorance, as their actions have laid bare the truth of their folly.

"We once called you 'judges,'" he laments on behalf of society, his voice tinged with disappointment. "But you have proven yourselves no better than the peasants you oppress, destined to fade into obscurity like all who came before you."

It is a sombre indictment, a reminder of the fleeting nature of power and the inevitability of its demise. Though they may wield authority for a time, their reign is but a fleeting illusion, destined to crumble beneath the weight of their own injustice.

And so, the ultimate judge pronounces his verdict, his words a harbinger of reckoning for those who have forsaken their sacred duty. In the end, they will be judged not by the accolades of men, but by the righteousness of their deeds and the compassion in their hearts.

It is with the above in mind we introduce you to the Child of Stalin. Firstly we will deal with some background material:

The scene is set

The Weight of a Name coupled with Bonds of Prejudice

In the small town of Margate, nestled on the South East Coast of England, lived a community that gave the appearance of being bound by familiarity and routine. Children appeared to play in the streets, neighbours exchanged what looked like pleasantries, and life echoed that of a gentle rhythm. Yet, beneath the surface of this idyllic facade, lurked the insidious tendrils of prejudice, waiting to ensnare the unsuspecting.

This could be said of many towns and villages of the UK after the influx of foreign settlers after the war years.

Among the residents of Margate were the Janowski family, with a father who, as a recent refugee from Siberia in Russia, fended for himself alone.

Pawel Janowski, a work avoiding gambler with a tendency towards everything dishonest and a violent demeanour, had moved to the town seeking a better life just for himself. His second son, Anthony, a bright-eyed boy with a passion for learning, quickly found himself drawn into the fold of the local schools.

However, despite efforts to integrate, the Janowskis found themselves the target of whispered rumours and sideways glances. It was the mere sound of their surname – Janowski – that seemed to trigger a cascade of unfounded assumptions and prejudices along with their appearance of having a very low social standing. It did not help that Mrs Janowski was suffering from Schizophrenia having been selected by Pawel to bear his offspring to secure his position as a permanent resident in the UK.

In the minds of the so-called respectable townsfolk of Margate, the name Janowski carried with it a heavy burden of history. Memories of Joseph Stalin, the infamous Soviet dictator, cast a long shadow over any individual with a Russian-sounding name. Though Pawel had never set foot in Moscow, with only a faint connection to Stalin, the townspeople couldn't shake the misguided association.

One particularly influential figure in perpetuating this prejudice was Mr. Thompson, a staunch conservative with a penchant for conspiracy theories. Convinced of a vast communist infiltration in the heart of the UK, he saw the Janowskis as the embodiment of his worst fears. "It's in their blood," Mr. Thompson would mutter to anyone who would listen, his voice dripping with disdain. "Stalin's spawn, lurking among us, waiting to strike."

His words found fertile ground in the minds of his fellow townspeople, many of whom were all too eager to latch onto any excuse for their own biases. And so, the Janowskis had become unwitting scapegoats for the sins of a bygone era.

For young Anthony, the weight of this prejudice bore down heavily upon his shoulders. Despite his tender age, he keenly felt the sting of ostracisation and exclusion. Classmates whispered behind his back, parents pulled their children away when he approached, and teachers regarded him with thinly veiled suspicion.

"Why do they hate us?" Anthony would ask, his eyes brimming with confusion and hurt.

Pawel would never even think to gather his son to his arms, or hold him close as if to shield him from the cruelty of the world outside. He would not be bothered to explain that they fear what they do not understand, Anthony would just have to conclude, later as an adult, that he must not let their ignorance dim the light within him.

And so, Anthony endured, with his spirit unbroken despite the constant barrage of prejudice. In the face of adversity, he clung to his mother, finding solace in the bonds of family and the resilience of the human spirit.

The prejudice against the Janowskis never did wane, it just slowly but surely eroded within Anthony's mind and formed an unyielding force of empathy and understanding towards others who were also discriminated against. Neighbours would never really venture to extend olive branches, classmates would sometimes reach out with tentative gestures of friendship, and yet Mr. Thompson would never find himself even begrudgingly acknowledging the humanity of those whom he had vilified.

And as for young Anthony, he grew to understand that the true measure of a person lay not in the name they carried or the sins of their ancestors, but in the kindness of their heart and the strength of their character. This contrasted with the usual mindset of judging the perceived offspring of former crooks as worse then the crooks they came from, but Anthony knew that in the end, it was not the prejudices of others that defined him, but the love and acceptance he found within himself and those who stood beside him having been spawned from the following events:

Pawel's origins:

As a selfish refugee from a Siberian gulag Pawel, changed his Ukrainian surname to a polish name to take advantage of the the Sikorski-Maisky Agreement which was concluded at the end of July 1941 between the USSR ambassador and the Prime Minister of the Polish Government-in-Exile, providing an opportunity to free hundreds of thousands of Polish citizens from labour camps and prisons. This pact enabled the establishment of Polish armed forces within the USSR, and strengthened the anti-Hitler coalition. By joining the Polish forces Pawel was able to escape to the UK from Siberia in 1942 due to this edict from Stalin, but only after joining the Anders army of Polish soldiers under British command, then marrying a coal miner's daughter from Nottingham, as a Bevin Boy and moving to London as a doorman in the Windmill Theatre as his sojourn moved on.

This was a man who, to get a better chance of remaining in the UK, impregnated a schizophrenic named Audrey, and used her insurance savings to get a divorce from his first wife Nelly so he could make a marriage bond legal.

Pawel, such a selfish gambling addict, that when his second son Anthony was fostered into a caring couple's home while Audrey was forced by Pawel into an asylum, he offered to give this expendable child away for £10, only to be heavily rebuked by Audrey, in a moment of clarity, as she would fight tooth and nail to prevent any such thing happening.

How would Anthony's life as the boy that Pawel did not need, turn out? The following is a first hand account of recollections from Anthony who today retains the strength of having been nurtured by the most loving mother a child could have ever had and by a scheming father who placed multiple challenges upon him along the way seeking to distract him from any chance of progress through his childhood and teenage years. How would his life turn out while being treated as the offspring of Stalin within a biassed society? Further to this, it is anyone's guess whether his father acquired his own values from an emulation of Stalin's reputation or his own ingenuity. So, was Pawel a child of Stalin? and was Anthony treated by his UK peers as if he was a child of Stain? You decide.

Chapter 1: The Selfish Refugee

Pawel's journey from the icy clutches of a Siberian Gulag to the bustling streets of Glasgow then Nottingham and London, was one marked by selfish ambition and a callous disregard for others. Born with the Ukrainian name Janowicz, he shed his past like a snake casting off its old skin, adopting the Polish name Janowski as he sought refuge in the ranks of the Anders Army under British command during the tumultuous days of World War II.

His escape from Siberia was a feat of cunning and opportunism, seizing the chance to flee due to an edict agreed to between the Polish General Sikorski and Stalin that allowed him to join the Polish forces as they carved a path through the chaos of war. In the aftermath, after having assaulted British officers under the guise of having a mental illness, he was finally demobbed in Glasgow in 1942 and Pawel found himself in Nottingham, a city teeming with life and opportunity, where he soon crossed paths with a coal miner's daughter named Nelly.

After whisking an already pregnant Nelly to London and ostracising her from her family, she married Pawel after bearing her child, left him to his gambling ways and moved to Hull when Pawel moved on to Audrey who suffered from Schizophrenia.

Their courtship was swift, fuelled by Pawel's charm and Audrey's youthful naivety. They married in haste, and for a time, it seemed as though Pawel had found the stability he craved. But beneath the surface, his selfish tendencies simmered, waiting for the perfect moment to reveal themselves.

Pawel's gambling addiction was the first crack in the facade of his newfound life. He squandered their meagre savings on games of chance, his lust for risk blinding him to the needs of his growing family. As Audrey's belly swelled with the promise of new life, Pawel's debts mounted, casting a shadow over their future.

After Pawel had fathered his first British child, it seems it was "Job done" as his tenure in the UK seemed much safer, although he still harboured fears of being found out about his name change in the Gulags and possibly caught by Stalin who controlled the USSR in the years after the war. He was in a situation where the Polish government as a satellite state of the USSR, were trying to get Poles, who had fought for the British, returned and punished as 'against the soviet cause', even though Poland was not technically part of the USSR and if that happened his former identity as a Ukrainian may be exposed and the thought of being back in Siberia would put him into a permanent 'fight or flight' position with anyone getting in his way just becoming fodder in his aftermath.

His attitude towards more offspring differed somewhat and when their second son, Anthony was born, Pawel's selfishness reached new heights. Faced with the responsibility of fatherhood towards another son, he recoiled, seeking solace in the chaos of his own making. Unable and unwilling to provide for his growing family, he made a fateful decision: to offer Anthony up for adoption, a pawn in his relentless pursuit of self-gratification.

Christopher and Emily, kind-hearted foster carers, welcomed Anthony into their home near Dover in Kent, with open arms, offering him the love and stability that Pawel would not provide. As they bid farewell to the one-year-old boy they had grown to cherish, Pawel's indifference was palpable, his gaze fixed on the horizon, his mind already racing ahead to his next gamble.

But Audrey would not be swayed. Faced with the prospect of losing her second son, she stood firm, refusing to let Pawel's selfishness dictate this fate. With steely resolve, she rejected his attempt to adopt Anthony for a mere £10 return, her voice a beacon of defiance in the face of his callousness.

As they drove away from Christopher and Emily's home, the weight of Pawel's betrayal hung heavy in the air. In the silence that followed, Audrey's eyes met Pawel's in a silent challenge, a reminder that she would not be broken by his selfishness, that she would fight tooth and nail to protect her family from the darkness that threatened to consume them.

And so, as they drove into the unknown, Pawel's selfishness remained a spectre haunting their every step, a reminder of the price they paid for daring to hope for something more than the hand that fate has dealt them. But in

Audrey's unwavering resolve, there was also a glimmer of hope, a promise that even in the darkest of times, love could still triumph over selfishness and greed.

Little did Anthony or Audrey know at the time, that two years later, Audrey would be forced to adopt her only daughter Vanessa who was fostered out and who Pawel was more determined to adopt into a wealthy home only to pester these new parents of Vanessa until they moved to Rhetford to get away from him. Pawel simply used the ensuing adoption hearing as an opportunity for a day out, exclaiming that if he did not get a day out of jail, he would oppose the adoption, thus showing how little he cared about his only known daughter and his wife's happiness. The implication is clear from an ensuing letter written to the child's social worker that he would support the adoption of his and Audrey's only daughter Vanessa if he could just gain 12 hours out of his jail cell. Little did he know that these letters, along with the record of refusing his son Anthony a place at a prestigious grammar school and attempting to sell him for £10 would be kept within a microfiche record, available for Anthony to review in later life.

Chapter 2: The Deception

In the summer of 1964, innocence collided with deception in the life of young Anthony. It was a day etched into his memory, a day when promises of adventure masked the sinister truth lurking beneath the surface. As the sun dipped low on the horizon, a car pulled up to their modest home—a rare occurrence in their secluded corner of the world.

Wide-eyed with wonder, four-year-old Anthony watched as his father Pawel emerged from the car, accompanied by a stranger. Pawel's smile, though forced, promised excitement and adventure as he beckoned Anthony and his siblings to join them for a ride. Without hesitation, they climbed into the car, their excitement tinged with uncertainty.

As they journeyed into the unknown, Anthony's mind buzzed with questions, but his voice remained silenced by the weight of his father's authority. Hours passed, and the car finally came to a halt outside a looming building—an orphanage disguised as a sanctuary. Confusion gripped Anthony's heart as Pawel ushered them inside, his assurances falling on deaf ears. It was a cruel trick, a ploy to rid himself of their burden while he pursued his own desires.

With tear-stained cheeks and trembling hands, Anthony clung to hope that this nightmare would soon end. But days turned into weeks, and weeks turned into months, trapping

Anthony in a cycle of abandonment and betrayal.

The following summer of 1966 brought a chilling sense of déjà vu as history repeated itself. Once again, Anthony and his siblings were torn from their home without a chance to bid their mother farewell. Pawel's deceit knew no bounds as he callously deposited them at the doorstep of another foster home, his heart as cold as the Siberian tundra from which he hailed.

But amidst the darkness, a glimmer of resilience flickered within Anthony's soul. With each passing day, he vowed to protect his siblings from the pain inflicted upon them by their parents' sins. Together, they forged a bond stronger than blood—a bond forged in the crucible of adversity.

Despite the constant upheaval, Anthony's spirit remained unbroken. Each new challenge only served to strengthen his resolve. And though scars from the past lingered, they were a testament to the enduring power of love in the face of adversity.

Chapter 3: A Son's Defiance

One fateful morning, the air in the small household hung heavy with tension, thick like a suffocating fog. Pawel and Audrey, once bound by love, now found themselves locked in a bitter argument. Audrey lay sick in bed, her frail form hidden beneath layers of blankets, while Pawel stood by the door, his voice dripping with bitterness and frustration.

"Come, boys," Pawel's words were cold and calculated. "It's time to leave your mother behind. She's too much of a burden for us to bear."

But Anthony couldn't bear to abandon his mother in her time of need. Despite his father's callous words, he could see the fear and confusion in Audrey's eyes. With a courage fueled by love, Anthony stepped forward, his voice trembling but resolute.

"I won't leave Mum," he declared, his gaze meeting Pawel's with unwavering intensity. "I'll stay with her, no matter what."

Pawel's anger flared at Anthony's defiance, his fists clenching in frustration. Yet, beneath the facade of rage, Anthony glimpsed something else—a hint of shame, a flicker of humanity.

In that moment, Anthony understood that his father's cruelty stemmed not from malice, but from his own pain and brokenness. And though he feared the consequences of his actions, he could not abandon his mother to face them alone.

With a heavy sigh, Pawel relented, defeat evident in the slump of his shoulders. "Fine," he muttered, barely audible. "Stay with her, then. But know that you'll regret it."

But Anthony paid no heed to his father's warning, for in that moment, he had made a choice—a choice born of love and loyalty. As he wrapped his arms around his mother's trembling form, he knew he had made the right decision. Love, he realised, was the most powerful force of all—a beacon of hope even in the darkest of nights.

As the years passed, Anthony carried the scars of his tumultuous childhood. Yet, amidst the chaos, he clung to the belief that one day, he would find the stability and love he craved. With courage and resilience, he faced the challenges ahead, determined to carve out a brighter future for himself and his siblings. For in the depths of his soul burned a flicker of hope—a light that would guide him through the darkest of nights.

Chapter 4: The Sanctuary of Numbers

In the idyllic town of Margate nestled among rolling hills and murmuring forests, resided a boy named Anthony. At just eight years old, Anthony's life was a tapestry woven with threads of both love and hardship. His mother, Audrey, possessed a gentle soul overshadowed by the haunting spectre of schizophrenia. Despite her affliction, she enveloped Anthony in a cocoon of love and warmth, providing him with a sanctuary amidst the tempest that raged within their home.

Yet, alongside Audrey's tender embrace lurked the shadow of Pawel, Anthony's father—a man whose heart was as frigid as ice, casting a pall of darkness over their family. His actions inflicted wounds that cut deep into the fabric of their lives. But amidst the turmoil and anguish, Anthony found solace in the world of numbers. A prodigy in mathematics, his mind was a labyrinth of equations and calculations, offering him refuge from the tumultuous seas of his reality.

Within the bustling halls of Salmestone Elementary School, Anthony found sanctuary in the orderly realm of mathematics. He immersed himself in textbooks, his intellect aflame with the thrill of discovery. With each problem solved, he felt a sense of triumph coursing through his veins. And when he received his first double gold star for a flawless maths test, his heart swelled with pride.

It was the day of his third triple gold star that shattered Anthony's world. He had approached the test with meticulous care, his pencil tracing each equation with precision. But as he scanned the results, his heart plummeted. One simple sum had been marked incorrect—an error he knew he could not have made. The teacher claimed he had written a "3" that resembled an "8," but Anthony recognized it as a facade, a ploy to placate the more affluent parents whose children vied for supremacy in the class rankings.

Fury surged within Anthony's chest as he confronted the injustice before him. He pleaded with the teacher, his voice trembling with emotion, but she remained unmoved. In her eyes, Anthony was merely another troubled child from a fractured home—a statistic to be brushed aside and forgotten.

Yet, Anthony refused to yield to despair. With a resolute determination burning within him, he vowed to prove his worth—not only to his teacher but to himself. Late into the night, he pored over his textbooks, his mind ablaze with determination. He knew that nothing would thwart his dreams.

For Anthony was more than just a troubled child from a broken home. He was a mathematical prodigy—a force to be reckoned with, a beacon of hope in a world veiled in shadows. Though the road ahead promised trials and tribulations, Anthony faced it with unwavering courage and resilience, his spirit unbroken by the injustices that sought to dim his light.

Chapter 5: The Sting of Poverty's Awareness

At the tender age of seven, Anthony found himself acutely aware of the harsh reality of poverty that cast a shadow over his young life. Despite his efforts to shield himself from the subject, his threadbare clothes and unkempt appearance betrayed his family's financial struggles more overtly than he realised.

One fateful day, Anthony eagerly joined an after-school pottery class, unaware that it would serve as a stark reminder of his impoverished status. As he moulded clay into a whimsical piggy bank, he basked in the joy of creation, oblivious to the impending blow to his fragile self-esteem.

Upon completing his creation, the instructor kindly suggested that Anthony could use the slot on the piggy bank to store his pocket money. Though meant as a gesture of encouragement, the innocent remark pierced Anthony's heart like a dagger. Rendered speechless, he stood in stunned silence for the remainder of the lesson, the weight of his poverty bearing down upon him with crushing force.

Another painful reminder of his family's financial strain came when the school initiated a holiday savings plan. Encouraged to deposit ten shillings a week, the other children eagerly embraced the opportunity to save for an exciting school trip abroad. Anthony, desperate to participate, appealed to his selfish father—a compulsive gambler whose sporadic generosity offered fleeting hope.

To Anthony's astonishment, his father provided the initial ten shillings, igniting a glimmer of hope within the young boy's heart. Yet, despite his fervent prayers for repeated acts of generosity, they never materialised. With each passing week, Anthony's dreams of joining his peers on the coveted school trip dwindled.

As the deadline for the savings plan loomed, Anthony's heart ached with sorrow. The realisation that he would be left behind while his classmates embarked on an adventure abroad weighed heavily upon him, casting a pall of desolation over his young spirit.

To compound his humiliation, Anthony's father, Pawel, demanded the return of the ten shillings he had initially provided—an act that left Anthony feeling utterly dejected and ashamed. Forced to retrieve the paltry sum, Anthony's sense of worth plummeted, reinforcing the bitter truth of his family's dire financial circumstances.

Yet, amidst the pain and humiliation, Anthony clung to a flicker of resilience. Though poverty threatened to define his existence, he refused to surrender to despair. With a quiet resolve burning within him, he vowed to overcome the obstacles that stood in the way of his dreams, determined to carve out a brighter future for himself, despite the harsh realities of his upbringing.

Chapter 6: The Weight of Broken Promises

At the tender age of ten, Anthony found himself thrust into the workforce, too young to work legally but desperate for a means to escape the suffocating grasp of poverty that choked his family. With determination etched into his young features, Anthony secured a job as a table clearer, dishwasher, and operator of a heavy-duty potato peeling machine, earning a modest wage of four shillings an hour—a meagre sum that represented a glimmer of hope amidst the darkness of his circumstances.

His father, a figure consumed by selfishness and deceit, promised to safeguard Anthony's earnings, pledging to bank his wages every week until Anthony had accumulated £100—a lofty goal that required 500 hours of backbreaking labour to achieve. Yet, Anthony toiled tirelessly, fueled by the promise of financial stability and the faint hope of a better future.

But when the time came to reclaim his hard-earned money from his father's clutches, Anthony's hopes were dashed by the cruel reality of his father's addiction. It became painfully evident that his father had squandered the funds, lost to the insatiable appetite of gambling—each pound frittered away on fleeting moments of false promise, leaving Anthony bereft of the fruits of his labour.

The betrayal cut deep, reminiscent of past wounds inflicted by his father's deceitful machinations. Memories flooded Anthony's mind—like the time he sold his cherished Raleigh Chopper bicycle for £10, naively believing his father's assurances of a better replacement. Instead, his father seized the money under the guise of securing a superior tape recorder, only to return home with a subpar model purchased on hire purchase—an illusion shattered within weeks as the device was repossessed, leaving Anthony empty-handed and disheartened.

Now, as Anthony watched his friend gleefully riding the Raleigh Chopper he had sold, the sting of betrayal bit deeper than ever before. He was left without a bike, without a tape recorder, and without the £10 he had sacrificed in pursuit of his father's empty promises.

Yet, amidst the wreckage of broken dreams, Anthony's spirit remained unbroken. Though battered and bruised by the callousness of his father's actions, he refused to surrender to despair. With a steely resolve burning within him, Anthony vowed to rise above the betrayal, determined to forge a path to a brighter future, guided by the unwavering strength of his own resilience.

Chapter 7: The Triumphs and Tribulations of Adolescence

At the age of eleven, Anthony found himself on the precipice of adolescence, navigating a world fraught with both triumphs and tribulations. The previous year had been marked by disappointment as he missed out on the school trip abroad, a dream dashed by the failures of his father, Pawel—a cunning and selfish deviant whose actions often left Anthony grappling with the repercussions.

However, a glimmer of hope emerged from the shadows in the form of Anthony's caring uncle, the compassionate brother of his schizophrenic mother, Audrey. Despite Pawel's shortcomings, Anthony's uncle stepped in, channelling the full

£18.70 into the school's accounts, ensuring Anthony could partake in the much-anticipated trip. With newfound optimism coursing through his veins, Anthony embarked on the journey with a mixture of excitement and trepidation.

Determined to make the most of the opportunity, Anthony utilised an advance payment from his uncle to purchase new attire from an ironically named shop, "Foster Brothers." Clad in fresh flannel trousers, a pair of more expensive flared trousers, and a smart cardigan, Anthony sought to shed the trappings of his poverty-stricken upbringing, desperate to avoid standing out among his peers.

However, fate had other plans as a small patch of tar stained Anthony's trousers during a leisurely afternoon on a French beach. Undeterred, Anthony adopted a posh accent and playfully referred to his classmates as "old bean," eliciting amusement and irritation in equal measure.

Despite the minor hiccup, the trip proved to be a transformative experience for Anthony. He unwittingly found himself in possession of a newfound wealth following a poker game among the boys, enabling him to indulge in souvenirs—including a large ornamental smoking pipe, a cherished memento of his time abroad.

Yet, Anthony's newfound prosperity did not escape the notice of his teacher, Mr. Bird, whose accusations of theft cast a shadow over Anthony's enjoyment of the trip. Only when the missing purse was miraculously found did Anthony find temporary reprieve from Mr. Bird's unwarranted suspicions.

Returning home, Anthony's elation was short-lived as he discovered the harsh realities awaiting him—a home devoid of electricity and a TV sold by his father in a futile attempt to alleviate their financial woes.

As Anthony returned from the school trip abroad, a sense of contentment settled within him. The experience had been a rare escape from the confines of his everyday life, a chance to explore new places and create lasting memories. Yet, amidst the glow of satisfaction, a dark cloud loomed on the horizon.

The joy of the trip was soon overshadowed by a bitter altercation with his brother, a petty squabble that escalated into a heated argument. In the heat of the moment, a prized souvenir—an ornamental smoking pipe—met its untimely demise, shattered into irreparable pieces. The loss left Anthony dismayed, the tangible reminder of his journey now reduced to mere fragments of shattered dreams.

As if the blow of the broken pipe wasn't enough, Anthony found himself subjected to further humiliation upon his return to school. Mr. Bird, ever eager to showcase the school's achievements, gathered the students for an assembly to relive the highlights of the trip through a series of projected photographs.

However, what should have been a moment of shared camaraderie quickly turned sour as Mr. Bird seized upon a photo depicting Anthony by the River Seine in Paris. With a cruel twist of humour, Mr. Bird mocked the river's murky waters, likening them to Anthony's presence and implying that he had somehow tainted the very essence of the iconic landmark.

The taunting remarks cut deep, plunging Anthony into a pool of embarrassment and shame. The laughter of his peers echoed in his ears, a stark reminder of his outsider status in a world where he longed to belong.

Despite the setbacks and indignities he faced, Anthony refused to be defeated. With each challenge, he found strength and resilience, determined to rise above the obstacles that threatened to hold him back. And as he navigated the tumultuous waters of adolescence, he clung to the hope that one day, he would emerge from the shadows, triumphant in his pursuit of a brighter future.

Chapter 8: The Dreamer's Basement

In the heart of Margate in Kent, where the sun cast long shadows and whispers of dreams mingled with the breeze, a young Anthony found himself drawn to a world of wonder and possibility. His own upbringing, marked by the harsh realities of a conniving father and a schizophrenic mother, left him yearning for the warmth and stability that seemed to elude him at every turn.

It was on one fateful afternoon that Anthony stumbled upon a sanctuary unlike any he had known before—a basement nestled beneath the bustling streets, where the echoes of laughter and the scent of creativity filled the air like magic. Here, in the loving embrace of

Dominic's home, Anthony found solace in the company of a boy whose world seemed to shimmer with promise and potential.

Dominic, with his stable and loving parents, inhabited a realm far removed from the chaos of Anthony's own upbringing. While his father played the organ and his mother hired out deck chairs, Dominic worked tirelessly in the basement, honing his skills in acting and directing with a fervour that bordered on obsession.

As Anthony watched in awe, Dominic manipulated figurines upon a miniature stage, weaving tales of adventure and intrigue with a dexterity that belied his tender age. In those fleeting moments, Anthony caught a glimpse of a future far beyond the confines of Margate—a future where Dominic's boundless imagination would carry him to heights he had only dared to dream of.

It was no surprise to Anthony when he learned that Dominic had secured a role in a Stanley Kubrick film—a testament to his prodigious talent and unwavering determination. And though their time together was brief, Anthony carried with him the memory of Dominic's boundless ambition, a reminder of the power of dreams to transcend even the darkest of circumstances.

For Anthony, Dominic's basement became a past memory of sanctuary—a place where the boundaries of reality melted away, and anything seemed possible. And though their paths diverged almost as quickly as they had merged, Anthony never forgot the lesson he had learned in that magical basement—that with enough passion and perseverance, even the loftiest of dreams could become reality

Chapter 9: The Quest for Opportunity

Despite the daunting challenges looming over his life, Anthony harboured an insatiable thirst for knowledge and a fierce determination that burned like a beacon within him. In the shadow of poverty that had plagued his family for generations, Anthony saw education as his escape route—a chance to break free from the shackles of circumstance and carve out a brighter future for himself.

When the opportunity arose for him to sit the 11+ test, Anthony seized it with both hands, viewing it as his ticket to a realm beyond the confines of his small-town existence. With unwavering resolve, he dedicated himself wholeheartedly to his studies, filling his days with tireless hours of revision and preparation. Every page turned, every equation solved, brought him one step closer to his dreams.

As the day of the test dawned, Anthony approached it with a quiet confidence, his heart buoyed by the hope of what lay ahead. Weeks passed in anxious anticipation until finally, the letter arrived bearing the news of his fate. With trembling hands, he tore it open, his eyes scanning the words with a mixture of disbelief and elation. He had passed the 11+ test with flying colors, his ticket to a place at the prestigious grammar school now within reach.

But Anthony's joy was short-lived as he shared the news with his family. Instead of the expected celebration, he was met with silence from his father, Pawel, whose face remained impassive. When Anthony broached the subject of enrolling in the grammar school, Pawel's responses were vague and evasive, shrouded in half-truths and excuses.

For years, Anthony puzzled over the mystery of why he had been denied the opportunity to pursue the education he had worked so hard to attain. While his friends moved on to higher education and promising careers, Anthony felt trapped in a cycle of stagnation, his aspirations stifled by the limitations of his circumstances.

It wasn't until Anthony stood on the cusp of adulthood that the truth finally came to light. A chance encounter with an old family friend unveiled the dark reality behind Pawel's actions. Driven by selfish desires and a misguided attempt to save money on a weekly bus ticket, Pawel had deliberately sabotaged Anthony's chances of attending the grammar school.

The revelation hit Anthony like a sledgehammer, filling him with a potent mix of anger and sorrow. He realised that his father's actions had robbed him of opportunities and dreams that he had fought so hard to achieve. But amidst the turmoil of emotions, Anthony also found a glimmer of liberation—a resolve to chart his own course, independent of the shadows that had long haunted his past.

With newfound determination, Anthony set out to pursue his aspirations with renewed vigour. Each setback only fueled his determination to rise above the limitations imposed upon him. As he ventured into the uncharted territory of his future, Anthony carried with him the unwavering belief that no obstacle, no matter how formidable, could extinguish the flame of his dreams.

Chapter 10: A Turn of Events

At just 12 years old, Anthony's life veered off course, plunging him into a reality he never could have foreseen. It all began innocently enough—a carefree morning spent with friends, the air alive with laughter and youthful energy. But as the day wore on and the sun dipped lower in the sky, Anthony found himself swept up in a whirlwind of events that would alter the course of his existence forever.

It started with a dare—a reckless challenge from a friend to partake in a mischievous escapade. The allure of adventure, coupled with the rush of adrenaline, proved too tempting for Anthony to resist. Without a second thought, he accepted, unaware of the grave consequences that lay ahead.

As he climbed onto the moped, a sense of unease settled in the pit of Anthony's stomach. Deep down, he knew that what he was doing was wrong, but the idea of the thrill of the moment drowned out his better judgement. With his heart pounding in his chest, he never could have imagined the series of events that would unfold.

Unbeknownst to Anthony, his friend carried incriminating evidence in his pocket—car keys that tied them to a larger crime. In a twist of fate, Anthony found himself in the wrong place at the wrong time, ensnared in a web of circumstances beyond his control.

Arrested and charged with "taking a conveyance" and "going equipped for theft," Anthony's protests of innocence fell on deaf ears. Faced with overwhelming odds and the stark realities of the legal system, his legal team advised him to plead guilty—a decision born out of desperation and the harsh truths of the world he inhabited.

Standing before the judge, Anthony felt the weight of the moment bearing down upon him. With a heavy heart and a sense of resignation, he uttered the words that sealed his fate. His plea of guilty echoed through the courtroom, a solemn reminder of the injustice that had befallen him.

Yet, even as the gavel fell and the sentence was handed down, Anthony refused to surrender to despair. Deep within his soul burned a flicker of hope—a steadfast belief that one day, justice would prevail, and his name would be vindicated.

Though the road ahead stretched long and arduous, fraught with obstacles and challenges, Anthony faced it with unwavering courage and determination. His spirit remained unbroken by the weight of his unjust conviction, fueled by the conviction that truth would ultimately triumph over adversity.

As he embarked on the journey ahead, Anthony carried with him the indomitable belief that the light of justice would shine through the darkness, illuminating the path to redemption and setting him free from the chains of injustice,

Chapter 11: The Misguided Joyride

At the age of fourteen, Anthony found himself caught up in a whirlwind of trouble that would forever alter the course of his life. It all began with a seemingly innocent act—a joyride with three of his closest friends through a gated and locked goods yard on the outskirts of Margate Seafront.

It was a warm summer evening when Anthony and his friends stumbled upon the goods yard, its towering fences and forbidding gates standing as a challenge to their youthful curiosity. With a sense of reckless abandon, they scaled the fence and slipped inside, the thrill of adventure coursing through their veins.

As they explored the maze of shipping containers and abandoned machinery, Anthony couldn't help but feel a sense of exhilaration at the thought of breaking the rules and defying the boundaries that had been placed upon them. And when they stumbled upon a van parked in a secluded corner of the yard, temptation got the better of them.

With a mischievous grin, Anthony and his friends climbed into the van, the engine roaring to life beneath their touch. And with a sense of freedom that only comes from youth, they set off on a joyride through the deserted yard, the wind rushing through their hair as they careened around corners and raced down narrow alleyways.

But as the night wore on and the adrenaline faded, the reality of their actions began to sink in. They realised too late that they were trapped within the confines of the goods yard, the gates locked tight against any would-be escapees.

In their panic, Anthony and his friends made a fateful decision—they purposely drove the van towards the wooded dead-end, thus showing they were not heading towards the locked gates and sought refuge in the shadows, hoping to evade capture. But their fortune ran out when the police drove towards them, responding to reports of suspicious activity in the area.

And so, Anthony and his friends found themselves in the back of a police car, their hands bound with handcuffs and their hearts heavy with fear. They were charged with "taking away a vehicle," a crime that carried serious consequences.

But as they sat in their jail cell, Anthony couldn't shake the feeling of injustice that gnawed at his conscience. He knew that they hadn't stolen the van—they had simply taken it for a joyride around a private piece of land, with no intention of causing harm or breaking the law.

As the days turned into weeks and the reality of their situation sunk in, Anthony and his friends grappled with the harsh consequences of their actions. They faced court hearings and legal battles, their futures hanging in the balance as they awaited their fate.

But through it all, Anthony remained steadfast in his belief that they had done nothing wrong. And though their joyride had landed them in hot water, he refused to let it define him. For Anthony knew that true strength lay not in the mistakes we make, but in the lessons we learn and the resilience we show in the face of adversity.

Chapter 12: The Art of Ink

Anthony's thirteenth year was marked by a daring adventure that left a permanent mark on his body and his spirit. It all began with a chance encounter in the heart of Brooksville—a small tattoo parlour tucked away in a forgotten alley, its walls adorned with colourful designs and swirling patterns.

With a heart pounding with excitement, Anthony stepped into the dimly lit parlour, his eyes wide with wonder at the sight of the intricate designs that adorned the walls. The tattoo artist, a grizzled man with a twinkle in his eye, greeted him with a knowing smile, his hands steady and sure as he prepared his tools.

Anthony, always one to seek out new experiences, found himself drawn to the idea of getting a tattoo. With a confidence that belied his age, he convinced the tattoo artist that he was eighteen, his tall stature and mature demeanour lending credence to his claim.

And so, with a sense of anticipation coursing through his veins, Anthony settled into the chair, his heart racing as the tattoo artist began to work his magic. With each prick of the needle, he felt a thrill unlike anything he had ever experienced before, his skin coming alive with the vibrant colours and intricate designs that adorned it.

The first tattoo—a simple bust of a flowered lady—seemed to spring to life beneath Anthony's skin, its delicate features dancing in the flickering light of the parlour. The second—a flowered scroll with his name emblazoned upon it—held a special significance, a symbol of his identity and his place in the world.

But it was the third tattoo that truly captivated Anthony—a large parrot that tucked its wings down his upper arm, its feathers ablaze with colour and life. As the tattoo artist worked his magic, Anthony felt a sense of exhilaration wash over him, a feeling of freedom and self-expression that he had never known before.

And so, with a sense of pride and accomplishment, Anthony left the tattoo parlour that day with three new tattoos adorning his arms—a testament to his bravery and his willingness to embrace the unknown.

As he returned to school, his classmates were enthralled by the colourful designs that now adorned his skin, their eyes wide with wonder as they traced their fingers over the intricate patterns. And though Anthony basked in their admiration, he knew that his journey with tattoos was far from over.

But it was during a return visit to the tattoo parlour that Anthony's addiction to ink was finally tempered by the wisdom of the tattoo artist. With a gentle hand and a knowing smile, the artist insisted that Anthony take a break, allowing his body to adjust to the changes wrought by the tattoos.

And though Anthony initially baulked at the idea, he soon realised the wisdom of the tattoo artist's words. For it was in that moment of reflection that Anthony found a newfound appreciation for the art of ink—a respect for its power to transform and to inspire, but also a recognition of the importance of moderation and self-care.

And so, with a renewed sense of purpose, Anthony embarked on a new chapter of his life—one marked not by addiction, but by a tempered respect for the art of tattooing, and a commitment to honour its beauty and its significance with every design that adorned his skin, but at the same time a realisation that being tattooed at 13 would be a mark or two for life.

Chapter 13: The Unjust Confinement

At the tender age of fourteen, Anthony found himself entangled in a web of injustice that would forever stain his perception of authority and law. It began with a simple utterance—a word spoken in jest, but twisted into a weapon against him.

It was a brisk afternoon when Anthony and his friend found themselves strolling through the streets of Brooksville, their laughter echoing through the air like music. But their carefree demeanour was shattered in an instant when they encountered a police officer on patrol—a stern figure with a badge gleaming on his chest.

In a moment of impulsive defiance, Anthony called out to the officer, addressing him as "Constable" with a playful emphasis on the first syllable. To Anthony, it was nothing more than a harmless jest—a lighthearted poke at the authority that loomed over him like a spectre. There were no other persons within earshot and the officer warned Anthony and his friend not to do that again. When the officer turned has back Anthony called out "constable" with an emphasis on the first syllable, again without any real chance that others in the vicinity could be offended. The officer was not pleased.

As the officer saw it differently, he seized upon Anthony's words with a ferocity that took Anthony by surprise, accusing him of deliberately emphasising the syllable to create a derogatory term that would incite a breach of the peace.

Suddenly, Anthony found himself facing a barrage of accusations and threats of arrest, his protestations falling on deaf ears as the officer painted a picture of a volatile situation on the brink of chaos—a scenario that existed only in the officer's imagination.

Faced with the prospect of arrest, Anthony made a split-second decision to protect his friend, owning up to the supposed offence in a bid to spare them both from the clutches of the law and with a conviction that he had not incited a potential riot, but just upset an officer of the law. But even as he was led away in handcuffs, Anthony couldn't shake the sense of disbelief that washed over him—a feeling of betrayal at the hands of those sworn to uphold justice.

In court, Anthony's ordeal only intensified as he faced a magistrate who seemed determined to make an example of him. When asked if he had emphasised the first syllable of the word "Constable," Anthony dared to question the absurdity of the accusation in such a way as to encourage the magistrate to give an example, only to be met with a torrent of anger and contempt from the bench.

And so, Anthony was sentenced to three months in jail—a punishment that far outweighed the supposed offence he had committed. But even as he languished behind bars, Anthony refused to surrender to despair. With a determination born of injustice, he fought tooth and nail to appeal his sentence, tirelessly seeking justice in a system that had failed him.

Although his appeal against the sentence was ultimately successful, with his sentence reduced to a mere ten days, the scars of his wrongful imprisonment would linger long after his release. For Anthony knew that true justice could never be served until those responsible for his suffering were held to account. Had he truly been guilty of potentially disturbing the peace, this would imply that the officer himself would have breached the peace due to Anthony's mischievousness. When the appeals month into the sentence the conviction issue was not even considered.

As he emerged from his ordeal, Anthony vowed to never forget the injustice he had endured—to never lose sight of the fight for fairness and equality that had been ignited within him. And as he stood on the threshold of a new beginning, he knew that his journey was far from over, but he would face it with courage and determination, no matter the obstacles that lay ahead.

Chapter 14: The Temptation of Easy Money

At the tender age of fifteen, Anthony found himself ensnared in the allure of quick riches. Surrounded by youths driven by reckless ambition, he succumbed to the temptation of burglary. Led by misguided camaraderie, Anthony and his companions embarked on a fateful journey into the realm of criminality.

Their target: a nondescript shop, oblivious to the impending intrusion. As Anthony, ignorant amongst his friends looked on, a clandestine operation unfolded beneath the surface. Unbeknownst to him, the basement of the shop had become a treasure trove ripe for plunder.

All that was required was for Anthony and another to spend time and money in the shop and whilst completing their purchases, two of the others went downstairs and out of the rear alley.

After their exploits, they retreated to Anthony's humble abode, a sanctuary overshadowed by his father's selfish compulsions and his mother's tender but troubled presence. Behind locked doors, they tallied the spoils of their illicit endeavour, counting out £220 each, a sum that tantalised with the promise of newfound wealth.

But fate had a cruel twist in store. A nod to the Police from one who seemed to be Anthony's closest friend shattered his illusions of prosperity. A trusted confidant who had not been involved in the heist, swayed by envy, betrayed him to the authorities. Before he could revel in his ill-gotten gains, Anthony found himself shackled by the chains of justice, arrested and convicted for handling stolen goods. When the police had come knocking they did not search his room, but went straight to a small draw, pulled it out and retrieved the remaining £180 of his share, but declared only £60 as handled by Anthony, which begged the question, was the day of capture a bonus day for the Police? and perhaps even for his so-called best friend. When the newspapers summarised the matter the total stolen was £300 short of the amount that had been shared out in Anthony's bedroom, although the Police had initially known the full amount as when they confronted Anthony with the theft, he owned up to the full amount which was initially recorded as the amount he was to be charged with until they dropped the charge to the handling of £60 of stolen cash. This further injustice, however did little to ease the sense of regret over his involvement in the whole affair.

As the dust settled, Anthony grappled with the weight of guilt and remorse. The shop owner's loss weighed heavily on his conscience, a stark reminder of the consequences of his actions. Though he had only indulged in a fraction of the stolen loot, the burden of complicity bore down upon him, haunting his every waking moment until it gradually subsided into a past memory.

Chapter 15: A Life Marked by Turmoil

Anthony's tumultuous journey through life had thus far born the scars of a fractured childhood, marred by insanity and uncertainty. Conceived into chaos, having teetered on the precipice of despair, he was a pawn in what seemed a game of fate.

From the tender age of one, Anthony's life had hung in the balance as his schizophrenic mother intervened to halt his sale. Yet, the spectre of separation loomed large, as he was whisked away from her loving embrace time and time again, cast into the unforgiving arms of foster care.

Amidst the chaos, Anthony's spirit remained unbroken. Refusing to be torn from his mother's side, he clung to her love as a lifeline in the storm. Despite the turmoil that engulfed him, Anthony's resilience shone through, a beacon of hope in the darkest of nights.

But the shadows of adversity continued to loom large. From false accusations to violent encounters, Anthony's path was fraught with obstacles at every turn. Despite his innocence, he found himself ensnared in a web of injustice, betrayed by those entrusted with upholding the law.

Yet, amidst the chaos and turmoil, glimmers of hope pierced through the darkness. He was one day, to be acquitted by a jury of his peers and vindicated by the truth, Anthony emerged from the crucible of adversity stronger than ever, his spirit unbroken by the trials of life.

16: The Quest for Redemption

Haunted by the ghosts of his past, Anthony embarked on a quest for redemption, seeking solace in the aftermath of his transgressions. As he grappled with the weight of guilt and remorse, he found himself at a crossroads, torn between the allure of easy riches and the pursuit of a higher purpose.

Reflecting on his misdeeds, Anthony gleaned invaluable lessons from the crucible of adversity. Though the allure of wealth had once beckoned him with its siren song, he now saw through its hollow promises, recognizing that true happiness could never be bought with ill-gotten gains.

Driven by a newfound sense of purpose, Anthony resolved to chart a different course, guided by the moral compass instilled by his mother's love. Though the road ahead was fraught with uncertainty, he faced it with courage and conviction, determined to atone for his past sins and forge a brighter future.

With each step forward, Anthony sought to make amends for the harm he had caused, striving to leave behind a legacy of redemption in the wake of his tumultuous past.

Though the scars of his journey would forever mark his soul, he embraced them as a testament to his resilience and strength in the face of adversity.

Chapter 17: A Life Unravelled

Anthony's life had always been a precarious balancing act, teetering on the edge of chaos and uncertainty. Born into a world where the whispers of his mother's schizophrenia and the shadow of his father's vengeful past loomed large, Anthony navigated a landscape fraught with pitfalls and obstacles at every turn.

Despite the love of his mother, whose tender heart struggled to make sense of the demons that haunted her mind, and the erratic affection of his father, whose vices threatened to consume him whole, Anthony found himself adrift in a sea of turmoil and despair.

As he grew older, the spectre of his father's gambling addiction and criminal past cast a long shadow over Anthony's own life, leading him down a path lined with temptation and danger. Two jail sentences, supervision orders, and a conditional discharge marked the milestones of Anthony's tumultuous journey—a journey fraught with missteps and mistakes that seemed to follow him like a shadow.

But it was the events of one fateful day that would irrevocably alter the course of Anthony's life—a day when a simple misunderstanding spiralled into a nightmare of violence and betrayal.

His headmaster, perhaps well-intentioned but ultimately misguided, sent a damning report to the court—a report that painted Anthony as abusive and unruly, a menace to society and himself. But the truth was far more complex, far more insidious than anyone could have imagined.

The ex-police officer turned teacher, fueled by his own insecurities and prejudices, had unjustly punished Anthony for a crime he did not commit—a crime born not out of malice, but out of a desperate plea for understanding and compassion.

As Anthony's raised hand was mistaken for a sign of guilt, the teacher's fury knew no bounds, and in a fit of rage, he unleashed a torrent of violence upon Anthony's unsuspecting frame. The sound of breaking teeth echoed through the classroom, a chilling reminder of the injustice that had been wrought upon Anthony's fragile soul.

And so, as Anthony found himself the subject of a care order, his future hanging in the balance, he clung to the flickering flame of hope that burned bright within him—a flame fueled by the unwavering belief that justice would one day prevail, and that the truth would set him free.

But as the shadows closed in around him, Anthony knew that the road ahead would be fraught with challenges and obstacles—a road that would test his resilience and his resolve, and force him to confront the demons that had long haunted his past.

Chapter 18: A Cry for Justice Chapter

The day came where he would be sentenced for receiving £60 when, in fact it had been £40 spent of £220 and In the hushed confines of the courtroom, Anthony's fate hung in the balance—a fate dictated not by the truth, but by the whims of those who held his future in their hands. As the magistrates peered down from their lofty perch, Anthony braced himself for the inevitable verdict—a verdict that would seal his fate and determine the course of his life for years to come.

But as the evidence unfolded and the tangled web of deceit began to unravel, a glimmer of hope pierced the darkness—a hope born from the courage of one young boy's refusal to be silenced, to be swept aside like so much dust in the wind.

The truth, it seemed, was a fickle mistress, shifting and changing with each passing moment. And as the ex-police officer turned teacher took the stand, his facade of authority crumbling beneath the weight of his own guilt and shame, Anthony found his voice—a voice that rang out like a clarion call in the silence of the courtroom.

With each word that spilled from his lips, Anthony painted a vivid portrait of the injustice that had been inflicted upon him—a portrait stained with the blood of broken teeth and shattered dreams. And as the echoes of his testimony reverberated through the chamber, a sense of righteous indignation swelled within the hearts of those who bore witness to his courage.

For Anthony, the courtroom became a battlefield—a battleground where truth and justice clashed with the forces of corruption and deceit. And though the road ahead remained uncertain, he knew that he would not walk it alone—that the strength of his convictions and the fire in his heart would guide him through the darkness, and lead him towards the light of a brighter tomorrow.

As the judge handed down his care order, a sense of defeat washed over Anthony—and not a sense of triumph born from the knowledge that he had stood his ground, although he refused to be silenced in the face of injustice. Although he should not have, he emerged from the courtroom, his head held high and his spirit unbroken, Anthony knew that no matter what challenges lay ahead, he would face them with courage and determination, and never waver in his quest for truth and justice.

Chapter 19: A Twist of Fate

As the care order loomed over Anthony's life like a dark cloud, he couldn't help but feel a sense of resignation wash over him. Despite his initial resistance to the idea of being taken into care, he couldn't deny the need and the possibilities it presented—particularly the chance to attend the grammar school he had been unfairly denied at the age of eleven.

With his brother already placed in care, Anthony knew that his own fate hung in the balance, tethered to the whims of a system that seemed determined to thwart his every ambition. But as the prospect of a care home placement beckoned, Anthony found himself torn between the comfort of familiarity and the promise of a brighter future.

However, fate had other plans in store for Anthony, as his father and a conniving court clerk conspired to manipulate the situation to their advantage. Together, they crafted a plan to deceive the authorities into allowing Anthony to remain at home under the guise of a shortage of available care places—a plan that ultimately succeeded in thwarting the intentions of the care order.

Though Anthony couldn't help but feel a twinge of relief at the prospect of remaining at home, he couldn't shake the nagging sense of unease that gnawed at the edges of his consciousness. For while the immediate danger of being taken into care had been averted, the long-term consequences of his father's machinations remained to be seen.

Chapter 20: A Fragile Facade

As Anthony settled back into the familiar routines of home life, a fragile facade of normalcy descended over the household—a facade that belied the simmering tension that lurked just beneath the surface. With the threat of the care order temporarily averted, Anthony's father breathed a sigh of relief, secure in the knowledge that his national assistance payments would remain intact.

But for Anthony, the illusion of stability was shattered by the harsh reality of his circumstances. Though he longed for the chance to pursue his dreams and carve out a better future for himself, he found himself trapped in a cycle of dysfunction and deceit—a cycle perpetuated by the very people who should have been his staunchest allies.

As the days turned into weeks, Anthony couldn't shake the feeling that he was running out of time—that with each passing moment, his chances of breaking free from the confines of his upbringing grew slimmer. And though he clung to the hope that someday, somehow, he would find a way to escape the shadows that threatened to consume him, he couldn't help but fear that his dreams would remain forever out of reach.

Chapter 21: A Desperate Gamble

As the weight of his circumstances bore down upon him, Anthony found himself teetering on the brink of despair—a despair born from the realisation that the odds were stacked against him, and that the cards had been dealt long before he ever had a chance to play the game.

But in the face of adversity, Anthony refused to surrender to defeat. With a steely resolve and a determination forged in the crucible of hardship, he resolved to defy the odds and carve out a path for himself, no matter the cost.

Yet fate had one final twist in store for Anthony, as a chance encounter with a police officer would set into motion a chain of events that would alter the course of his life forever. Charged with the offence of swearing at an officer, Anthony found himself once again thrust into the unforgiving embrace of the justice system—a system that seemed determined to crush his spirit and extinguish the flame of hope that burned within him.

But even as he stood on the precipice of despair, Anthony refused to back down. With the strength of his convictions as his guide, he vowed to fight tooth and nail for the chance to reclaim his future and defy the odds that threatened to consume him.

For Anthony knew that while the road ahead might be fraught with obstacles and challenges, he would never surrender to the darkness—not as long as the flame of hope burned bright within his heart, lighting the way towards a brighter tomorrow.

Chapter 22: The Care Order's Deception

As the care order loomed over Anthony's life like a dark shadow, he couldn't shake the feeling of uncertainty that gripped his heart. The prospect of being placed into care, away from the familiar comforts of home, filled him with dread and apprehension. Yet, little did he know the true extent of the deception that awaited him.

The court order had been meticulously worded to place Anthony initially into the care of the police, which was a harsh reality that he couldn't escape. But when the clerk of the court sidestepped this directive with a cunning manoeuvre, citing "no available spaces,"

Anthony found himself caught in a web of deceit that would shape his future in ways he could never have imagined.

Despite the fact that he technically remained in the care of the police, Anthony was allowed to return home under the guise of a lack of placement options. The clerk of the court's manipulation of the situation allowed Anthony to slip through the cracks of the system, avoiding the fate of institutionalisation that had loomed so menacingly before him.

But as Anthony settled back into the familiar routines of home life, a gnawing sense of unease lingered in the back of his mind. Something didn't feel quite right about the way his care order had been handled, and he couldn't shake the feeling that he was being kept in the dark about something sinister lurking beneath the surface.

Little did Anthony know, the very system designed to protect him had failed him in the most egregious of ways, as the local social services feigned compliance with the care order, fabricating paperwork to make it appear as though Anthony had been in their care for years—a deception that would have far-reaching consequences for Anthony's future.

Chapter 23: The Illusion of Normalcy

With the immediate threat of being placed into care seemingly averted, Anthony breathed a sigh of relief as he settled back into the familiar rhythms of home life. But beneath the facade of normalcy, a storm was brewing—a storm of deceit and manipulation that threatened to tear Anthony's world apart.

As the days turned into weeks and the weeks into months, Anthony couldn't shake the feeling that something was amiss. The care order, once a looming spectre that haunted his every waking moment, had faded into the background, replaced by the illusion of normalcy that had settled over his life like a thick fog.

Yet, despite the outward appearance of stability, Anthony couldn't shake the feeling that he was being kept in the dark about something sinister lurking just beneath the surface. The fabricated paperwork and feigned compliance of the local social services painted a false picture of Anthony's circumstances, obscuring the truth of his precarious situation.

But as Anthony delved deeper into the tangled web of deception that surrounded him, he began to unravel the threads of deceit that had ensnared him. With each revelation, the illusion of normalcy shattered, revealing the harsh reality of his circumstances in stark relief.

Chapter 24: The Weight of Deception

As Anthony grappled with the weight of deception that had been thrust upon him, he found himself teetering on the edge of despair—a despair born from the realisation that the very system designed to protect him had failed him in the most egregious of ways.

The fabricated paperwork and feigned compliance of the local social services painted a damning portrait of the lengths to which they would go to conceal the truth of Anthony's circumstances. It was a betrayal of trust that cut deep, leaving Anthony reeling from the realisation that he had been kept in the dark about the true extent of his situation.

But amidst the turmoil and uncertainty that surrounded him, Anthony refused to succumb to despair. With a steely resolve and a determination forged in the crucible of hardship, he vowed to uncover the truth and reclaim control over his own destiny.

Armed with the knowledge of the deception that had been perpetrated against him, Anthony set out on a journey of self-discovery—a journey that would lead him to confront the demons of his past and forge a path towards a brighter future.

For Anthony knew that while the road ahead might be fraught with obstacles and challenges, he would not walk it alone. With the strength of his convictions as his guide, he would navigate the treacherous waters of deception and emerge victorious, reclaiming his autonomy and his rightful place in the world.

Chapter 25: The Midnight Ride

The seafront was shrouded in darkness as Anthony toiled away behind the counter of a take-away burger and fries joint, the scent of grease and fried food hanging heavy in the air. His eyes flickered anxiously towards the window, where his prized XS 650cc Yamaha motorcycle stood parked, a silent sentinel against the night.

As the clock struck midnight, Anthony locked up the shop and grabbed two crash helmets, eager to escape the monotony of his shift and feel the wind whipping through his hair as he rode along the deserted streets. His friend eagerly hopped onto the back of the bike, anticipation shining in his eyes as they roared off into the night.

But their joyride was short-lived, as the sound of screeching tires and flashing headlights shattered the stillness of the night. An unmarked car bore down on them, its headlights blazing with menace as it barreled towards them with reckless abandon.

Anthony's heart hammered in his chest as he realised they were being pursued, the roar of the engine drowned out by the pounding of his pulse. In a panic, he flicked off the bike's headlights, hoping to evade their pursuers in the darkness.

But fate had other plans, as a faulty indicator stubbornly remained lit, casting a damning glow that betrayed their position to their assailants. Desperate for refuge, Anthony spotted a cordon of police officers stationed near Margate Football Club, their presence offering a glimmer of hope in the darkness.

With a surge of relief, Anthony steered towards the "safety" of the officers, his heart pounding with the promise of salvation. But as they approached, his hopes were dashed in an instant, as the unmarked car careered towards them with lethal intent.

In a flash of chaos and violence, Anthony and his friend realised they had been chased by an unmarked police car and found themselves under attack by more officers, their helmets ripped from their heads as blows rained down upon them with brutal force. Anthony's refusal to remove his full-face helmet only seemed to enrage their attackers further, as they beat him mercilessly with their truncheons.

For what felt like an eternity, Anthony was trapped in a nightmare of pain and confusion, his world reduced to a blur of flashing lights and bloodied fists. But as suddenly as it had begun, the onslaught came to an end, leaving Anthony battered and bruised, but defiant in the face of his attackers.

As he emerged from the chaos, Anthony was filled with a sense of outrage and betrayal, his faith in the system shattered by the brutality he had endured. And though he was eventually released without charge, the scars of that fateful night would haunt him for years to come, a reminder of the dangers that lurked in the shadows, ready to pounce when least expected.

When you bear the above in mind, consider the ethics of how Anthony has been treated.

He would be the first to acknowledge that his challenging behaviour needed to be restrained and that as much as his mother would have preferred him to have avoided trouble at school or with the authorities, she had no power of discipline while Pawel ruled with an iron fist and to make it worse, Pawel's discipline only suited himself as and when Anthony and his brother interfered with Pawel's own selfish pursuits. There was no long term gai to be had by grabbing a belt and unleashing his vile temper in anger simply because Athony had been to the beach and lost a shoe in the mud, but that is how Pawel was when any form of unnecessary expense was placed upon him.

The idea of responsibility and reward was not something Pawel had ever considered and when it came to something like buying their first bikes, it was inevitable that the hire purchase loan company would, after a couple of weeks of non-payment, take these fickle gestures away from the boys.

This pattern would repeat itself when their pet dog was apparently 'lost' or 'ran away' and in time it was found that it was more than likely abandoned due to the responsibility of purchasing dog food.

So when Anthony and his brother walked out of a store with water pistols they had not paid for at the age of 7 and 8, it would be no surprise that when caught they would make the mistake of being caught by a police officer. Then, as this was their first venture into crime, they would be more frightened of upsetting their so called father and so gave a false address, only to be rumbled by the rather obvious name of Janowski which in the seaside town of Margate in the 1960s was so rare that it was inevitable that a visit to their home would ensue.

What was a very bad lesson was that when the police arrived to give them a warning, having previously retrieved the water pistols, Pawel was far more concerned about giving some sort of impression that he was a 'good' father and in front of the officer he handed over a pound for the boys to share.

In his heart of hearts Anthony knee this was a flawed approach and for the first time, although relieved that the belt was not used, realised that this was a very bad lesson, that if caught stealing their father may even reward them.

How could children, given this type of encouragement, be expected to follow the straight and narrow path of honesty. And so, stealing as a wrong would have to be learned the hard way, by being caught by the police countless times in the future as this vital lesson had not been learned.

Anthony would have to use his own sense of right and wrong, hindered by Pawel's distorted views that sometimes led to Pawel defrauding Anthony of his savings earned by picking whelks from age 9, climbing chimney stacks at 10, clearing tables, peeling potatoes and chipping them and washing dishes from the age of 12.

Anthony never really knew that his abusive father was doing anything that was not for the benefit of his schizophrenic mother and did not make the calculation that with the correct use of his time and resources Pawel could and should have engaged in washing dishes of peeling potatoes or picking whelks. Anthony accepted that Pawel could not find work, however obvious it became that he squandered his time at the bookies of gambling halls or snooker tables.

Pawel showed that all he was concerned about was making a life for Pawel despite what would result for his family, and on top of this he seemed to actively be involved in scuppering Anthony's progress wherever that may manifest itself.

When Anthony excelled in rounders, the idea of encouraging this sport pursuit did not enter Pawel's head or when Anthony broke the school record at high jumping by being one of the few in Kent to master the new Frosby flop as opposed to the straddle. Pawel could have encouraged Anthony to pursue this sport which he loved, but Pawel was likely more aware of the black or red of a roulette table.

Anthony knew that on any given Saturday Pawel could recall the results of any given horse race that day to any punter that wished to know a result, but had far less success naming the winner before the race.

Chapter 26: The Parking Debacle

As Anthony's van rolled into the unmarked parking area, he found himself unwittingly stepping into a legal quagmire. The absence of a conspicuous entry sign, hinted at a bureaucratic maze lying in wait.

Obligated to halt, the driver glanced over at the side where a parking conditions sign stood, a beacon of perplexity rather than clarity.

In a bid to comply, the driver's next move would logically have to be a choice of: applying for a permit online or seeking assistance via phone. Yet, both avenues were bound to lead to dead ends. The online system languishes in dysfunction, and the phone will only ring unanswered, echoing futile attempts at any resolution.

No accord to park had materialised, with no agreement inked. The van stood as a token of unwitting trespass, its owner, Anthony, being unknowingly left ensnared in an imminent legal web.

UK Car Park Management Ltd, an entity wielding more power and wealth than Anthony, swiftly pounced with a relentless fervor, chasing Anthony with demands down corridors of bureaucracy.

Despite Anthony's previous attempt to lawfully transfer liability to the company who had control of the vehicle, the relentless pursuit persisted for over two years, as a sterile and circular task within the realm of administrative absurdity.

Letters penned by Anthony, brimming with rationale and pleading, met a formidable adversary in the form of corporate might. It seemed a déjà vu of past injustices, reminiscent of the bias faced due to his foreign name and apparent ignorance.

The absurdity of the situation underscored the nightmarish nature of this bureaucratic overreach.

The case lingered, a shadow over Anthony's daily existence. A civil claim loomed on the horizon, its outcome uncertain.

A precedent, Janowski v DPP, whispered of hope, suggesting that fundamental defects could unravel the claimant's case.

Yet, as the wheels of justice ground forward, the transfer of liability confirmed by the claimant languished in obscurity. A new parking charge notice bore the company's name, not Anthony's, a glaring oversight ignored by their relentless pursuit of profit.

For a judge to rule against Anthony this would necessitate a dismissal of reason, a disregard for justice. The absence of an entry sign, the void of a grace period—each a testament to the absurdity of the situation and a valid transfer of any mistaken liability.

Updates are currently awaited and a promise of resolution in a later edition. Whatever the outcome, a record would endure within this publication bearing witness to a contest with bureaucratic implications.

To be continued.................

A further edition will explore Anthony's
exploits as he:

Carefully avoids the trap of drug addiction

Overcomes the tendency to drink too much

Switches jobs to take on courses in motor
mechanics

Sues a large retail chain, wins, only to have
the judgement wrongfully overturned

Sues the Police for assaulting his father,
exposing their complicity

Struggles to protect his mother despite his father's aggression

Curtailed the negative effect of his father's addiction to gambling

Becomes embroiled in a legal dispute with a multinational corporation

Has judicial sanctions placed on him by the attorney general halting his ability to litigate

Creates bad case law before the President of the Queen's Bench Division

Notes that the same bad case law mysteriously disappears from public archives

Takes on a private criminal prosecution

sanctioned by the Chief Magistrate of
England Penelope Anne CBE Hewitt

Experiences the local Margate Magistrates
dispensing with the same matter without
even a hearing

And other exploits that expose the justice
system's flaws

The concept of the 'Child of Stalin'
disposition exists in many ways, in that if an
individual can be falsely associated with a
negative historical entity, then there becomes
a direct correlation between this stigma and

how far the authorities and the judicial system can go to hound these individuals into submission.

Yet if the same individuals use the judicial process to attempt to 'right the wrongs' he/she will create a lasting record of matters that, if read directly from the court records, leave the judicial process as openly exposed for all to read.

The above matters did happen and there is a paper and microfiche trail of judgements, social services records, war records and newspaper clippings to substantiate the history of this 'Child of Stalin'.

Sponsored by The Best Beano Cafe'

1 Dane Road, Margate great google reviews nice family run cafe' treating people as they find them and very friendly with good food at fair prices.

People who treated Anthony with fairness

Published by Antbooks ©

info@green-day.co.uk

.

Printed in Great Britain
by Amazon